THE
GRANDPARENT'S BOOK
OF SHARED MEMORIES

A family chronicle prepared by

....

....

Sharing Your Story

The simple pleasures of family life are oftentimes will-o'-the-wisps—aglow for the moment but evaporating all too soon. This memory book/photo album allows you, as grandparents, to preserve your reminiscences for posterity. Reader's Digest provides the framework as you provide the stories and pictures.

- The *All About Us* section is devoted to you—your childhood, your marriage, the arrival of your children, and your day-to-day family life.
- The *Our Children* and *Our Grandchildren* sections are provided for you to record fond memories of family members individually and as a whole.
- The *Our Ancestors* pages let you document interesting individuals from earlier generations of your respective families.
- Two *pocket pages* hold mementos ranging from school report cards to your wedding program to ancestors' letters or documents.
- The booklet *Exploring Your Family History,* tucked into the inside back cover, will help you find distant forebears and leaf out the family tree.

WRITING IT DOWN

You might see this album as a loving record of a long-complete extended family or an unfolding work-in-progress. Likewise, when writing about yourselves and your family you may welcome the suggestions found in the lined pages or ignore them.

In any case, it's a good idea to write drafts of your stories until they meet your satisfaction, then leave them for a day or so and reread them. After adding any final touches, transcribe your words onto the album pages. Your reward? A retrospective of family life treasured for generations to come.

A NOTE TO RECORD KEEPERS The paper in this album is lignin-free and acid-free, meaning it will not yellow over time nor damage the photographs you choose to display. Accompanying the album are adhesive photo corners that will keep your family pictures in place.

ALL ABOUT Us

"Someone said that God gave us memory so that we might have roses in December."

—J. M. Barrie

{ GRANDMOTHER }

About *Me*

Give some thought to what you'd like your grandchildren to remember about you—
what has interested you the most over the course of the years, your favorite activities
and pastimes, your opinions and beliefs, or anything else you'd like to share.

Name

Nickname

Date of birth

Place of birth

Hometown and residences

How I would describe myself

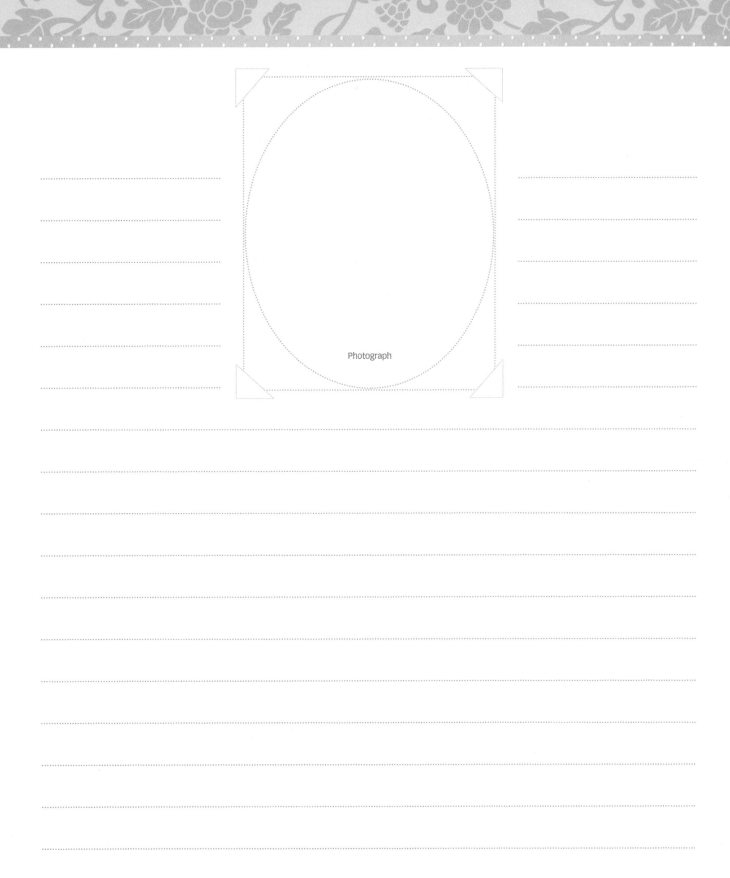

Photograph

My Mother

Name .... Nickname ....

Date of birth .... Place of birth ....

Hometown and residences ....

....

MEMORIES OF MY MOTHER ....

....

....

....

....

....

....

....

....

....

Photograph

"Our fathers had their dreams; we have ours; the generation that follows have their own."

—Olive Schreiner

My Father

Name

Nickname

Date of birth

Place of birth

Hometown and residences

MEMORIES OF MY FATHER

Photograph

My Brothers and Sisters

Name .... Nickname

Date of birth .... Place of birth

MEMORIES OF ....

....

....

....

....

....

Name .... Nickname

Date of birth .... Place of birth

MEMORIES OF ....

....

....

....

....

Name .... Nickname ....

Date of birth .... Place of birth ....

....

MEMORIES OF ....

....

....

....

Memory Box

List the books and toys
you and your siblings
enjoyed the most, the
games you played, and
any other favorite things
that come to mind.

❖ ....

❖ ....

❖ ....

❖ ....

❖ ....

❖ ....

❖ ....

When I was *Young*

What are your memories of life as a toddler and schoolgirl? Or of your hometown, friends, and childhood pursuits? These kinds of recollections are sure to catch your grandchildren's interest.

Where I lived

MEMORIES FROM TODDLER TO TEEN

"Youth looks forward but age looks back."

-----British proverb

Photograph

My School Days

Memories of school friends, teachers, and activities grow more fond as the years go by. After-school activities (such as music lessons and sports practices) and memories of the "what I did on summer vacation" sort could also be recorded on these pages.

ELEMENTARY SCHOOL TO JUNIOR HIGH

Schools attended   Location   Years

Schoolwork and activities

Memory Box

List a couple of classroom subjects in which you excelled and some that weren't your cup of tea.

* ....
* ....
* ....
* ....

"Youth has no age."
----Pablo Picasso

HIGH SCHOOL AND BEYOND

Schools attended   Location   Years

Schoolwork and activities

Diplomas/Degrees

Work and Community Life

Whether you worked outside the home or managed the household, you surely have stories to share. You can also use these pages to record your participation in clubs or organizations and any military or volunteer service you performed at home or abroad.

WORK LIFE

MILITARY/VOLUNTEER SERVICE

"Work apace, apace, apace, apace;
Honest labour bears a lovely face."
—Thomas Dekker

MEMBERSHIPS/COMMITMENTS

Photograph

Along the Way

Write about your memorable stops on the road to adulthood. Don't hesitate to be personal as you recall memories and your growing perception of the world at large.

LESSONS LEARNED

ACCOMPLISHMENTS/AWARDS

....

....

....

....

WORLD EVENTS I'LL ALWAYS REMEMBER ···

....

....

....

....

....

....

....

....

....

....

My *Favorite Things*

What you like to do the most says a lot about you. Use these pages to note your favorite pastimes and recreational activities (whether playing golf, cooking, reading, moviegoing, or traveling), and anything else that comes to mind.

ACTIVITIES AND PASTIMES

FAVORITE BOOKS AND MOVIES

FAVORITE EXPRESSIONS ···

···

···

···

SIMPLE PLEASURES ··

···

···

···

Memory Box

Note your favorite foods or
dishes; they can be meals
you or your husband cook
yourself or you enjoy when
eating out.

❖ ···

❖ ···

❖ ···

❖ ···

❖ ···

❖ ···

❖ ···

Reflections

Use these pages to reflect on your coming of age, "the way things were" in your youth, and any memories, thoughts, and bits of wisdom you wish to share with your grandchildren.

....

....

....

....

....

....

....

....

....

....

....

....

....

....

Memory Box

Recall women's fashions of your youth—short shorts, mood rings, and the like—and what was "all the rage" at one time or another.

❖ ....

❖ ....

❖ ....

❖ ....

❖ ....

❖ ....

❖ ....

❖ ....

❖ ....

{ GRANDFATHER }

About Me

Give some thought to what you'd like your grandchildren to remember about you—
what has interested you the most over the course of the years, your favorite activities
and pastimes, your opinions and beliefs, or anything else you'd like to share.

Name   Nickname

Date of birth   Place of birth

Hometown and residences

How I would describe myself

Photograph

My Mother

Name

Nickname

Date of birth

Place of birth

Hometown and residences

MEMORIES OF MY MOTHER

Photograph

"A mother understands what a child does not say."

-----Jewish proverb

My Father

Name .... Nickname ....

Date of birth .... Place of birth ....

Hometown and residences ....

....

....

MEMORIES OF MY FATHER ....

....

....

....

....

....

....

....

....

....

Photograph

My Brothers and Sisters

Name .... Nickname

Date of birth .... Place of birth

MEMORIES OF ....

....

....

....

....

....

Name .... Nickname

Date of birth .... Place of birth

MEMORIES OF ....

....

....

....

....

Name

Nickname

Date of birth

Place of birth

MEMORIES OF

Memory Box

List the books and toys
you and your siblings
enjoyed the most, the
games you played, and
any other favorite things
that come to mind.

When I was *Young*

What are your fondest memories of your life as a youngster? Or of your hometown, friends, and favorite childhood activities? These kinds of recollections are sure to catch your grandchildren's interest.

Where I lived

MEMORIES FROM TODDLER TO TEEN

"Youth would be an ideal state if it came later in life."

—Herbert Henry Asquith

....

....

....

....

....

....

....

....

....

....

....

Photograph

....

GRANDFATHER

My School Days

Memories of school friends, teachers, and activities grow more fond as the years go by. After-school activities (such as music lessons and sports practices) and memories of the "what I did on summer vacation" sort could also be recorded on these pages.

ELEMENTARY SCHOOL TO JUNIOR HIGH

Schools attended   Location   Years

Schoolwork and activities

Memory Box

List a couple of classroom subjects in which you excelled and some that weren't your cup of tea.

◆ ....

◆ ....

◆ ....

◆ ....

◆ ....

HIGH SCHOOL AND BEYOND

Schools attended	Location	Years

Schoolwork and activities

Diplomas/Degrees

GRANDFATHER

Work and Community Life

Whether you worked in an office, a plant, or in the great outdoors, you surely have stories to share. You can also use these pages to record clubs or organizations in which you were active, along with military or volunteer service at home or abroad.

WORK LIFE

MILITARY/VOLUNTEER SERVICE

"Work is an essential part of being alive."

----Kay Stepkin

MEMBERSHIPS/COMMITMENTS

Photograph

Along the Way

Write about your memorable stops on the road to adulthood. Don't hesitate to be personal as you recall memories and your growing perception of the world at large.

LESSONS LEARNED

ACCOMPLISHMENTS/AWARDS

"We turn not older with years, but newer every day."

----Emily Dickinson

....

....

....

....

WORLD EVENTS I'LL ALWAYS REMEMBER ....

....

....

....

....

....

....

....

....

....

My *Favorite* Things

What you like to do the most says a lot about you. Use these pages to note your favorite pastimes and recreational activities (sports, traveling, reading, or moviegoing), and anything else that comes to mind.

ACTIVITIES AND PASTIMES

FAVORITE BOOKS AND MOVIES

FAVORITE EXPRESSIONS

SIMPLE PLEASURES

Memory Box

Note your favorite foods
or dishes; they can be
meals you or your wife
prepare at home or you
enjoy when eating out.

❖
❖
❖
❖
❖
❖
❖

Reflections

Use these pages to reflect on your coming of age, "the way things were" in your youth, and any memories, thoughts, and bits of wisdom you wish to share with your grandchildren.

....

....

....

....

....

....

....

....

....

Memory Box

Recall men's fashions of your youth—skinny ties, madras bermuda shorts, and the like—and what was "all the rage" at one time or another.

❖ ....

❖ ....

❖ ....

❖ ....

❖ ....

❖ ....

❖ ....

❖ ....

❖ ....

....

....

....

....

....

How We Met

Two became one at some point, but how did it happen? When and where did you meet? Share with future generations the story of how the two of you came to start a new life together.

Our Engagement and Wedding

....

....

....

....

....

....

....

....

....

Photograph

....

Our First Years Together

Struggling newlyweds or on easy street from the beginning? Your descendants will be eager to hear how it all began. Talk about your early years as husband and wife.

WHERE WE LIVED

City/Town   Years

City/Town   Years

City/Town   Years

MEMORIES OF LIFE AS NEWLYWEDS

*"There is no more lovely, friendly, and charming relationship,
communion or company than a good marriage."*

—Martin Luther

....

....

....

....

....

....

....

Memory Box

Jot down the cities, towns,
or recreation areas you
visited in the early years
of your marriage, whether
you stayed close to home
or ventured farther afield.

❖ ....

❖ ....

❖ ....

❖ ....

❖ ....

❖ ....

❖ ....

❖ ....

Becoming Parents

Learning that you'll be welcoming a new member of the family and preparing yourself for the blessed event . . . Recapture those wonderful memories here.

"WE'RE EXPECTING!"

Photograph

"Mother's arms are made of tenderness, and sweet sleep blesses the child who lies therein."

-----Victor Hugo

REMEMBRANCES OF THE SOON-TO-BE PARENTS

PREPARING FOR THE NEW ARRIVALS

Becoming Parents

Life changes forever once a baby arrives, and even more so as the family grows. Remember what it was like to be new parents and share those memories with your children and grandchildren.

THE BIG DAY ARRIVES

Photograph

FIRST DAYS AT HOME

Becoming Parents

GETTING THE HANG OF IT

"Fatherhood is the single most creative, complicated, fulfilling, frustrating, engrossing, enriching, depleting endeavor of a man's adult life."

----Kyle D. Pruett

THE JOYS OF NEW PARENTHOOD

The Social Side

Has your social life revolved around partygoing or the occasional quiet dinner with friends? And what about community and sports events, clambakes, or nights out at the pub? Tell all, if you like!

MEMORABLE DINNER PARTIES

MEMORABLE FUNCTIONS AND CELEBRATIONS

OTHER SOCIAL ACTIVITIES

Family Friends

"You gotta have friends," the song goes, and truer words were never spoken. On these pages you can record memories of friends from far and wide and what they mean to you and your family.

Name(s)

REMINISCENCES

Name(s)

REMINISCENCES

*"It is chance that makes brothers
but hearts that make friends."*

—Von Geibel

Name(s) ....

REMINISCENCES ....

....

....

....

....

....

Memory Box

List friends with whom
you've traveled and
note where and when
you went.

❖ ....

❖ ....

❖ ....

❖ ....

❖ ....

❖ ....

❖ ....

❖ ....

Family Friends

Name(s)

REMINISCENCES

Name(s)

REMINISCENCES

Fond Memories

Fun times and periods of togetherness are almost always documented in photographs, but stories of escapades and memorable moments during these occasions can speak volumes.

FAMILY VACATIONS

HOLIDAYS AT HOME

"The family—that dear octopus from whose tentacles we never quite escape."

—Dodie Smith

FAVORITE FAMILY ACTIVITIES ....

....

....

....

OUR PETS ....

....

....

....

....

....

....

....

....

Photograph

[OUR LIFE TOGETHER]

Fond Memories

FAMILY GATHERINGS ···

REMINISCENCES OF FAVORITE RELATIVES ···

OUR CHILDREN

"Give a little love to a child, and you get a great deal back."

— John Ruskin

First Years

What was your child like as a baby and preschooler? Recall when your baby's personality emerged. What were his or her treasured objects, favorite toys, and developing interests?

MEMORIES ....

*"Blessed be childhood, which brings down something
of heaven into the midst of our rough earthliness."*

—Henri-Frederic Amiel

FAVORITE THINGS

Memory Box

Your child's first steps…his or her first words.
List these and any other noteable firsts.

❖ ....

❖ ....

❖ ....

❖ ....

❖ ....

❖ ....

❖ ....

Childhood

Reminisce about your child's primary interests, such as music, dance, sports, scouting, and reading. You could also brag about any memorable accomplishments and recall your child's best friends.

Activities and interests

Talents/Accomplishments

Friends

School Days

Summarize your child's journey through school—beginning at kindergarten—recalling high (and not-so-high) points or anything else you'd like to record.

....

Schools attended	Location	Years

Schoolwork and Diplomas/Degrees

....

....

....

....

....

....

All Grown Up

Talk about the path your child took after his or her school days and where the path led—working nine-to-five, bound for adventure, raising a family, or living the single life.

Home life

Occupation

How I would describe...

....

....

....

....

....

....

....

Favorite memories

....

....

....

....

....

....

[ALL ABOUT ....]

First *Years*

What was your child like as a baby and preschooler? Recall when your baby's personality emerged. What were his or her treasured objects, favorite toys, and developing interests?

....

MEMORIES ....

....

....

....

....

....

....

....

....

....

....

....

"The childhood shows the man,
As morning shows the day."

-----John Milton

FAVORITE THINGS

Memory Box

Your child's first steps…his or her first words.
List these and any other notable firsts.

❖ ....

❖ ....

❖ ....

❖ ....

❖ ....

❖ ....

❖ ....

ALL ABOUT ....

Childhood

Reminisce about your child's primary interests, such as music, dance, sports, scouting, and reading. You could also brag about any memorable accomplishments and recall your child's best friends.

Activities and interests

Talents/Accomplishments

Friends

School Days

Summarize your child's journey through school—beginning at kindergarten—recalling high (and not-so-high) points or anything else you'd like to record.

....

....

Schools attended   Location   Years

....

....

....

....

....

Schoolwork and Diplomas/Degrees

....

....

....

....

....

All Grown Up

Talk about the path your child took after his or her school days and where the path led—working nine-to-five, bound for adventure, raising a family, or living the single life.

Home life

Occupation

How I would describe...

....

....

....

....

....

....

....

Favorite memories

....

....

....

....

....

....

First Years

What was your child like as a baby and preschooler? Recall when your baby's personality emerged. What were his or her treasured objects, favorite toys, and developing interests?

....

MEMORIES ....

....

....

....

....

....

....

....

....

....

....

....

....

"Child of love, our love's expression,
love's creation, loved indeed!"

—Ronald S. Cole-Turner

FAVORITE THINGS

Memory Box

Your child's first steps…his or her first words.
List these and any other notable firsts.

❖ ....

❖ ....

❖ ....

❖ ....

❖ ....

❖ ....

❖ ....

[ALL ABOUT

Childhood

Reminisce about your child's primary interests, such as music, dance, sports, scouting, and reading. You could also brag about any memorable accomplishments and recall your child's best friends.

Activities and interests

Talents/Accomplishments

Friends

School Days

Summarize your child's journey through school—beginning at kindergarten—
recalling high (and not-so-high) points or anything else you'd like to record.

....

....

Schools attended	Location	Years

....

....

....

....

....

Schoolwork and Diplomas/Degrees

....

....

....

....

....

{ ALL ABOUT .... }

All Grown Up

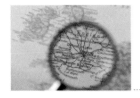

Talk about the path your child took after his or her school days and where the path led—working nine-to-five, bound for adventure, raising a family, or living the single life.

Home life

Occupation

How I would describe...

Favorite memories

Reflections on Parenthood

What are your thoughts on parenting and who your children have become?
Follow the suggestions below or let your memories take wing.

What we love most about parenting

What our kids have in common and how they differ

*"'Mid pleasures and palaces we may roam,
Be it ever so humble, there's no place like home."*

----John Howard Payne

....

....

....

....

....

....

Proudest moments

....

....

....

....

....

....

....

Reflections on Parenthood

Lessons we taught our children

What our children taught us

A Word from our Children

Turnabout is fair play, so here is your children's chance to pen favorite memories of their activities, adventures, and tender moments with *you*.

How we would describe our parents

Favorite memories

OUR GRANDCHILDREN

"If I would have known that grandchildren were going to be so much fun I would have had them first."

—Bill Laurin

First Impressions

Relive the thrill of meeting your grandchildren for the first time.
What were your feelings and impressions?

Name

Date of birth   Place of birth

Name

Date of birth   Place of birth

Name

Date of birth   Place of birth

"Behold the child, by Nature's law,
Pleas'd with a rattle, tickled with a straw…"
----Alexander Pope

....

....

Name

....

Date of birth   Place of birth

....

....

....

Name

....

Date of birth   Place of birth

....

....

....

Name

....

Date of birth   Place of birth

....

....

....

Our Grandkids as Toddlers

Describe your young grandchildren as parts of a beautiful whole—and because they'll likely be reading this, make sure you give each one equal time!

....

All About ... *(name)*

....

....

....

....

All About ... *(name)*

....

....

....

....

All About ... *(name)*

....

....

....

*"A grandchild fills a space in your heart
that you never knew was empty."*

—Anon.

SPECIAL MEMORIES ....

Memory Box

Many of the places you took your grandchildren probably made their eyes grow wide—a museum, the circus, the county fair. Jot down a few of the most memorable excursions.

❖ ....

❖ ....

❖ ....

❖ ....

❖ ....

❖ ....

❖ ....

❖ ....

❖ ....

Grandkids' School Days and *Beyond*

Yes, they're growing up in a flash! In fact, they already may be adults with children of their own. On this page and the following two, describe the people your grandchildren have become.

All About ... *(name)*

All About ... *(name)*

"Another thing 'so simple a child can operate' is a grandmother."

—Anon.

All About ... *(name)* ....

....

....

....

....

....

....

....

All About ... *(name)* ....

....

....

....

....

....

....

Grandkids' School Days and *Beyond*

All About ... *(name)*

_____

_____

_____

_____

_____

_____

All About ... *(name)*

_____

_____

_____

_____

_____

_____

Allow Us to Brag

Let go and praise your grandkids to the skies—they're not like anyone else. Here's your chance to note their brilliance, sparkling personalities, good looks and hidden talents.

The superstar named...

The superstar named...

The superstar named...

"No cowboy was ever faster on the draw than a grandparent pulling a baby picture out of a wallet."

—Anon.

The superstar named...

The superstar named...

The superstar named...

Thoughts on Being a *Grandparent*

Becoming a grandparent is a rejuvenating experience and a beautiful example of the natural order of things. How has being a grandparent enriched your life? This page and the two that follow let you reflect on how your life has been changed by the latest generation.

"Nobody can do for little children what grandparents do. Grandparents sort of sprinkle stardust over the lives of little children."

—Alex Haley

Thoughts on Being a *Grandparent*

....

....

....

....

....

....

....

....

....

....

....

....

....

....

OUR ANCESTORS

"Poor is the rich man who knows not from whence he came, and the faire lady with no thread to the past."

—Anon.

Grandmother's *Great Grandparents*

Whether you remember your great grandparents very well or they had passed on by the time you were born, write what you know of them here.

....

MY GREAT GRANDMOTHER ....

....

Name

....

Date of birth   Place of birth

....

What I remember or know of her

....

....

....

MY GREAT GRANDFATHER ....

....

Name

....

Date of birth   Place of birth

....

What I remember or know of him

....

....

....

Grandmother's Great-Great Grandparents

Any information that you have on your great-great grandparents will be of interest to your family and can aid in tracing your roots.

MY GREAT-GREAT GRANDMOTHER

Name

Date of birth   Place of birth

What I remember or know of her

MY GREAT-GREAT GRANDFATHER

Name

Date of birth   Place of birth

What I remember or know of him

Interesting Ancestors on My Side

Stories of distant forebears may have been passed down in your family, or perhaps you've come across interesting ancestors while researching your family history. Keep their stories alive by recording the details on these pages.

Name

Date of birth   Place of birth

Name

Date of birth   Place of birth

"Ancestors are the bark of the family tree."

—Anon.

....
Name

....
Date of birth   Place of birth

....

....

....

....

....
Name

....
Date of birth   Place of birth

....

....

....

....
Name

....
Date of birth   Place of birth

....

....

....

Grandfather's Great Grandparents

Whether you remember your great grandparents very well or they had passed on by the time you were born, write what you know of them here.

....

MY GREAT GRANDMOTHER ....

....

Name

....

Date of birth   Place of birth

....

What I remember or know of her

....

....

....

MY GREAT GRANDFATHER ....

....

Name

....

Date of birth   Place of birth

....

What I remember or know of him

....

....

....

Grandfather's *Great-Great Grandparents*

Any information that you have on your great-great grandparents will be
of interest to your family and can aid in tracing your roots.

MY GREAT-GREAT GRANDMOTHER

Name

Date of birth   Place of birth

What I remember or know of her

MY GREAT-GREAT GRANDFATHER

Name

Date of birth   Place of birth

What I remember or know of him

Interesting Ancestors on My Side

Stories of distant forebears may have been passed down in your family, or perhaps you've come across interesting ancestors while researching your family history. Keep their stories alive by recording the details on these pages.

Name

Date of birth   Place of birth

Name

Date of Birth   Place of birth

"Every man is a quotation from all his ancestors."

-----Ralph Waldo Emerson

....
Name

....
Date of birth   Place of birth

....

....

....

....

....
Name

....
Date of birth   Place of birth

....

....

....

....
Name

....
Date of birth   Place of birth

....

....

....

The Story Continues

Close this album of memories as you wish, writing about your relationship with your grandchildren and their parents, reflecting on life in general, your hopes for future generations—whatever suits your fancy.

"Bliss in possession will not last;
Remembered joys are never past."
—James Montgomery

The Story Continues

"To me old age is always fifteen years older than I am."

----Bernard Baruch

The Story Continues

"Age is opportunity no less
Than youth itself, though in another dress,
And as the evening twilight fades away
The sky is filled with stars, invisible by day."

—Henry Wadsworth Longfellow

"Our children are here to stay, but our babies and toddlers and preschoolers are gone as fast they can grow up— and we have only a short moment with each. When you see a grandfather take a baby in his arms, you see that the moment hasn't always been long enough."

— St. Clair Adams Sullivan